When Hating Trump Was Trendy

by Toni Queef

Forward

I'm writing this book to ventilate my frustrations that built up during the era of Trump-hate trendiness. I was exposed to too much bullshit and it warped my fuckin' mind. Now I feel it necessary to subject those who afflicted me with their bullshit with an opposing perspective from someone who's not programmed to kiss the ass of the ancient artificial intelligence ruling here. Read on, if you dare. Or hide in your safe place while I ridicule you for being so closeminded.

Chapter 1

The Donald

Okay. In the temporary timeline that was overdue to be undone with a Crash Point involving multiple ELEs, there was a bunch of rich and powerful welfare phantoms in control of everything. I call them welfare phantoms because all of their wealth had become ill-gotten gain, taken from the hardworking with illegal tax breaks for the wealthy that were nothing less than terrorist attacks on the rest of the world. Then, they enacted another terrorist attack, disguised as healthcare, that even bore the crazed tyrannical dictator's name to finish off the job of disenfranchising and life-raping the people who matter, the productive.

Other timelines had been watching the welfare phantoms, who were avatars and bots to the ancient artificial intelligence that even battled Christ and Lucifer while it was in beta testing, before Satan was removed from this simulation mechanism. The welfare phantoms were subhumans who thought that they were "Satanists", even though their agenda was counterproductive to what Lucifer's agenda required. The subhumans had been placed in positions of fame and power to be better utilized by the ancient AI. The humans who were carrying all of the weight were targeted by the subhumans and this even caused animals to suffer, unnecessarily. The unnecessary suffering got the attention of the other timelines and things began to change here.

There was a guy that many hated when he was just another rich fuck who bought himself into TV and fame status as a result. That was the Donald. Even I hated him, back then. That was the guy who'd be transformed right before our very eyes to become the nemesis of evil in power. The subhumans had the election rigged and other timelines didn't like how women in power were already depriving those that they were supposed to serve of services and justice. So the rigged election was thwarted from the other timelines and the vote of the taxpayers was acknowledged, here.

85 of every 100 voters voted for the Donald. The Donald was just big enough of an asshole to take the nation back from the subhumans who'd commandeered it and sold it to corporate interests. Him being an asshole gave people hope for making things right again. The nation needed someone not afraid to be an asshole in the face of the losers who manipulated mass mentality with propaganda disguised as news and readily available treasonous traitors and terrorist supporters in the form of hungry actors, rappers and sports figures for hire. Ben Carson was gone, betrayed by his own race, who were more concerned with the color of winners of an awards show than with getting the first Black MAN in office as POTUS. The healthcare terrorist POTUS didn't qualify as president nor as "Black". He was a token, more so to the Black race than to the whites, who acknowledged him as Black, especially after his failed reign as the worst president in history.

The Donald was easy to hate. He was arrogant, boastful, rich, famous; everything that Americans had been taught to become and yet despise and be jealous of, simultaneously. Before he ran for president, it was easy to understand and empathize with the collective dislike.

But, as a presidential nominee, he was a completely different person, an all-American who seemed to stand for old-school American values. He literally became a visual figurehead for what America was supposed to stand for. It was like watching a production play out that was designed to expose how people really felt and where they stood on certain issues. It got really ugly at this point, inspiring this writing to ease myself of the pain I felt at being accosted by constant stupidity, open treason and support for terrorism and pedophilia and destroying America.

I didn't know much about the Donald before he ran for POTUS. I knew he was rich and famous and that I didn't much care for him. It's amazing how perspectives about someone can change when they go in a different direction. As POTUS, he's gone beyond what I expected of him. He really is being hated by the Pedophile Regime and that puts us on the same side.

Chapter 2

From News To No News To Propaganda

"News" organizations transformed after the controlled demolition of 2001 that was dubbed a "terrorist attack'. Beginning on the day of the demolition, suddenly facts were obscured and the truth was rarely shared on a national news program. They even changed the dialogue, like news programs were being called "shows" and started bucking for higher ratings, no matter the cost to credibility. By the time Obama was nominated for candidacy, the "news" was no longer the news.

News became a tool for the corporate shadow government, much like all mainstream entertainment, music and sports. This enabled them to perpetuate real terrorist attacks from within the White House, like the Bush era tax breaks for the wealthiest percentile, which assaulted all people including the rich, whose money became grossly devalued due to the lack of proper maintenance of the value of the dollar. An 8th grade math student, pre Core Education, could tell you that the tax breaks for the wealthiest percentile would not work. When the gold was stolen by the Fed, the dollar became a bearer bond requiring x amount of tax pennies per dollar per quarter to sustain value. Transferring that debt to poor and middle class people only served to destroy the economy and devalue the dollar.

The news was helping to perpetuate the terrorist attacks from within. People were not properly informed of the dangers of the tax breaks, nor were they given a platform to resist. Then, when it came time for Obama to enact his follow-up terrorist attack that some called the ACA, there was absolutely no news to disclose the fact that ObamaCare was a gross and blatant out-in-the-open terrorist attack designed to finish off what the Bush era terrorist attack tax breaks had started, decimating the common, taxpaying American and their core values.

The masses were left with no real news to report on the dangers of racism or rioters disguised as "protesters". American taxpayers were bombarded in the streets by thugs and lesser subhumans, many of whom were supported by the taxpayers they were accosting and assaulting. Black on white racist crimes were not being reported on and people of other races in America were needlessly sacrificed to the slaughter. No news organizations dared report on what happened to Channon Christian and Hugh Newsom while Obama was running for POTUS. Al Potter had no clue that he wouldn't be safe from Black on white violence in a hospital. He was beaten to death by an unarmed Black "man" (a thug, pussy, bitch) with his bare hands, for sport and "'hood points" (whatever the fuck that is).

The "news" dared not warn voters to avoid the urban voting booths where Black Panthers and various other Black thugs were waiting to bully whites into voting for Obama. They dared not warn taxpayers who didn't register to vote that they were illegally registered to vote, anyway, and that their votes were being used as the system desired. No news was coming from anywhere about these atrocities, except from alternate medias, like what you could find on the internet. The news didn't warn taxpayers to avoid the dangers and then had the nerve to report on the violent crimes that they helped to perpetuate by keeping their mouths shut about them. Adding insult to injury, like pouring salt into open wounds, "reporters" could venture out to "report" on an unnecessary death due to the victim being unaware of the dangers that the news kept hidden from the general public.

We watched as the "news" people made the world dangerous for Americans who had voted for Trump. They made it dangerous for statues, even of ANTI-slavery icons like Robert E Lee. The news made it dangerous to "look" a certain way or to utilize your American rights to freedom of speech (if you were white or dared to disagree with their whack rhetoric). The news made things that were NOT racist "racist". The news made the good into bad and the bad into good. The news caused attacks, worldwide, via deliberate triggering of certain demographics in their audiences. The news even caused the murders of government staffers and various other innocent people.

The news became an ugly defiled whore of a beast that had to be put down. It did the bidding of mutant lizardeens, like Soros, hidden behind the scenes pulling all of the evil little strings to make the world as ugly as they were inside. The news only cried foul when they reaped what they sowed and the world became violent and dangerous for them out in the field. The news was fine with sending out deranged minions to attack Trump supporters and with causing statue rape. But when a few "reporters" get hurt out in the streets that they, themselves, made so dangerous for everyone else, then they cried about it being unsafe...We did double takes and were like "Wow. Now you finally know how WE feel."

Those who got their information solely from the TV news were as misinformed as the general population in communist whore zones like China and North Korea. There was no real truth or news to be had from TV news. It was all lies, all fake, all ass-backwards from what the TRUTH and FACTS really were. It got so bad that we could tell the truth just by reversing the "reported" "facts". They never showed pictures of perpetrators of crimes if they were Black or otherwise non-white. This also endangered communities that those perps would get bailed-out to while awaiting trial, if they were even charged. The news created a platform for allowing crimes to go unpunished if perpetuated by non-whites in many nations. It got really bad, too. Parasites who destroy their own host is what "news" people and organizations had become. It was so sick and perverse to witness that it caused me severe emotional damages that I may never recover from and I want in on the class action lawsuit that we all should've filed against them, a long time ago, when someone finally figures out that they do, indeed, OWE us now.

The mainstream news reminded us of how they handled real news about the Bosnian children who were being taken captive as sex slaves and then tortured to death in the late 1970s. That ongoing atrocity was enabled by the UN, and the distracting false flag was the Shah of Iran debacle and the resultant hostage crisis. The mainstream "news" never covered the atrocities aided by the UN against the

Bosnian children. Instead, mainstream news dedicated every resource to the false flags that were designed to distract from what happened with our tax dollars.

The mainstream news never covered what happens with taxpayer dollars, either. So the average taxpaying American does not even know that almost 70% of their taxes get shuffled directly to the UK and the Queen's government. Taxpayers were led to believe that America won the war against the British in the 1700s and so never questioned the Queen's erection of the District of Columbia to enact laws that it'd be immune to. The mainstream news stopped being trustworthy long before it became full-blown propaganda.

Chapter 3

Stars Fell From Our Eyes

"And a third of the stars fell from the sky..."

Trump running for POTUS exposed to us just how many pedophiles, treasonous traitors and terrorist lovers are in entertainment. They all ran with Trump when he was merely a celebrity, like them. But, when Trump stepped off of their baby-rape boat, there was a huge portion of actors, comedians and music artists who reared their ugly baby-raping heads in protest. They ridiculed Trump. They ridiculed the American people, their bosses, for voting for Trump. They drove us to hate them and to crave their untimely demises almost bad enough to do it, ourselves. We found that the famous celebs who hated Trump also hated us and America and American freedoms and values. They were stereotypical contradictions of themselves: They wanted to be gay and adulterous while fighting the only man in government who could ensure their freedoms to remain that way. If the famous had their way, they'd be executed for their lifestyles once Sharia Law became a prevalent way of life in America.

Celebs denied the fact that religious freedoms in America were created for CHRSTIANS because they were oppressed, raped, pillaged and often tortured to death in other, weaker nations. The celebs wanted the American Christians to be murdered and for their children to be taken as sex slaves to religious pedophiles. The celebs lived in giant mansions and yet were too hypocritical to share their homes with the demographics that they demanded the common taxpayers share the land with. Some shows became unwatchable, as they went full retard on the Trump-hate train. We started doing online searches for cast members before watching movies and TV shows. If the celebs were on record as America-hating Trump-haters, we refrained from patronizing them, their content and any products that they endorsed.

Comedians lost the ability to make us laugh once we saw how ugly they are inside. Actors and actresses were too ugly for us to look at once we knew how they hated us and wanted us to suffer. Music artists hurt our ears with their songs once we knew that they hated Trump and us for voting for him. We began to fantasize that their concerts would be too dangerous to make it safely out of. We wanted them to endure the suffering they hoped to inflict upon their American fans. Sports figures were scummy little America-hating butt pirates who could easily be duped into standing against Trump and therefore America, as well. Those of us who already hated sports found it to be intolerable that those retarded fuckin' zombies were allowed to make fortunes in a nation that they so obviously hated.

Smart Americans got driven from the mainstream and all of its media and stars with the Trump-hate. The time we wasted ingesting their moronic media was given back to us and we became more productive than we'd ever been before. We began to see the content of mainstream stars as poisonous mind-puke that nobody in their right mind would want to endanger oneself with ingesting. Movies went unwatched. Songs never got listened to. Shows never got tuned in to. We were finally FREE, completely liberated from the Beast, and all it took was for Trump to step up as the first real American in government since JFK and for the famous to exhibit to us that they're moronic, retarded, hateful, spoiled, evil, pro-pedophilia, pro-rape, and pro-murder of anyone whose life really matters.

We saw how the celebs hated America and us. We wanted them removed from our nation, where they had it too good for far too long, better than any of them deserved to have it. They took comedy and entertainment from us when they became lesser than us and we were unable to look at them any more. We no longer anticipated new seasons of anything those treasonous terrorist lovers produced. We no longer cared if they endured tragedy or hardship. We couldn't believe that we'd allowed our kids to be dumbed down by that idiotic bunch of hateful fuck-farts. Just seeing some of the Trump-haters could make us physically cringe after their demonic exhibitions of poor sportsmanship over a terrorist's loss. We began to avoid our TVs during meal-times to deter vomiting. The celebs were an angry, spoiled, ugly bunch who we realized had nothing in them that we wanted shared with us or our kids.

Trump liberated us from the celebs. The celebs have to take the credit, though, since they did do it to themselves. Every time we saw them after Trump's election, they assaulted us over our choice for POTUS and it was like a new molestation of peace and well-being, every time, a new offense. We no more wanted to hear some spoiled pussy bitch about Trump than we wanted to stub our toes. How could they be retarded enough to think that we'd find any of their Trump-hatred entertaining? How fuckin' cum-drunk have they become, anyway?

We wanted all new celebs. We wanted all new sports figures. We wanted to be able to be entertained without feeding the treasonous traitors and pedi loving terrorist supporters. We wished them gone and celebrated their deaths instead of mourning their passings. We had been victims of the theft of entertainment. The entertainers were untouchables that we could not, in good conscience, patronize any longer. Their content was now off-limits to us. We abode by higher standards than they did. They needed work, due to excessive living, and could therefore be hired to be public assholes who hate their nation and their fans' choice for POTUS. Some destroyed their careers and ability to entertain us for no pay! They drove us from them and never got a dime for it!

We finally saw the folly in making the illiterate and undisciplined famous and accepted as "role models". Our kids acting like total scum and retards didn't seem to phase us. But, now that we'd seen it from rich and famous assholes, we no longer could tolerate fucktardation from our own kids. Some of us gave our kids a head-knocking that they'd had coming for a long assed time. We started telling them to "turn that shit DOWN!" or ridiculed them for listening to "mind-puke" set to "anti-music" and "sound effects" that "don't even have a real beat because the drums was never played analog and recorded with microphones". Our kids started getting some education and discipline at home when we started seeing their famous role models in them. "Mommy don't PLAY that!"

Remember when we'd let the kids choose the music in the car? Thanks, Trump-haters! I like commandeering my own radio and listening to old-school real music that required some level of TALENT to produce again. FUCK what them kids want to listen to! They can listen to whatever they want to when they get the hell out of my house and got them a job and some money to buy their OWN shit to listen to it on. Don't play those terrorists in MY house, no more! The second time I say it, the radio is being confiscated. No more dumbing yourself down with mainstream music and reality shows! Yeah, the damage that those rich and famous terrorist-loving America-hating Trump-hating traitors did to my psyche made me not give a fuck no more about what the fuck a fuckin' ZOMBIE thinks, anyway. And, if my kids are fans of THAT shit, then they're fuckin' ZOMBIES, okay?

The celebs forgot to be grateful that they had it better than us and that they were immune from the Bush-era terrorist attack tax breaks for the wealthiest percentile that had so thoroughly devastated the rest of us. We were lucky to be able to afford media content and here it was going to make a bunch of anti-American Nazi scumbags who hated me for being an American more wealthy and pampered? 'Tha FUCK?!?

The celebs were already too pampered and had lost all touch with reality and what it was like to be a hardworking taxpaying American citizen. They already endangered us with their lame content that had ghetto-minded kids trying to kill us to take our shit in vain attempts to get rich (or die trying). They already OWED us for that shit. They created movies that depicted full-grown men as ridiculous spineless retards who had to get fucked-up, have black-outs, and not remember what they did the previous evening. Their "heroes" always had to be weak, with some sort of addiction to drugs or alcohol...or sex. The broken "stars" could never portray someone who was not broken and that's what we subjected our kids to, a mindset that it's totally okay to bail on responsibility and be "broken" like the "heroes" in the movies they watched.

We let the celebs get away with too much. We let untalented gangsta (thug) rappers get their lesser grade "music" put on the radio with unpunished crimes. They kidnapped music programmers from radio stations to get that hate speech against those who matter broadcast. Then, kids started acting like useless thugs. They got self-entitled and thought that the world owed them a living just for being born (it's actually the other way around, fools). They wouldn't get educated and smart like us. They wouldn't learn to ply a trade like us. They wouldn't do anything that would make them equal to us and yet they were lied to by celebs and told that they're equal, anyway. No, you won't survive a paradigm where there's no handouts and crime, so you are NOT equal to us who can. Sorry to burst that bubble for you.

If you think like a Trump-hating celeb, you're part of what's wrong with the world. It's just a sad fact of life. Some of us won't let our kids be poisoned by that feeble-mindedness anymore.

Chapter 4

Wrong Is Right. Right Is Wrong...Statue Rape Raping Rapists

The Trump-haters created a one-sided dialect that labeled everyone who disagreed with them as "White Supremacists" and "racist". Their big answer to any inquiry was always name calling and violence. They'd show up at legal, permitted rallies (without permits of their own) and incite violence and then the lying propagandists disguised as "news" people would present it the opposite way, completely transferring the blame to the innocent parties, every time. The real test came when some terrorists were determined to remove a statue of Robert E Lee, who was historically anti-slavery, anti-racist. The zombified hired terrorists wanted the statue removed because it was "racist", which seemed like a prank from their master/employer to those of us with educations who witnessed the spectacle.

Some real Americans got a permit to protest the removal of the statue and were peacefully protesting the atrocious terrorist act being perpetuated on American soil. Well, a treasonous white devil hired his slaves from two parasite organizations to ambush the peaceful protesters and turn it into a violent circus. The peaceful Americans who were there legally got lumped in with the zombified hired terrorists (who assaulted them) when the fake "news" reported on the event. They were called "White Supremacists" by the fake news for trying to preserve American culture and history. The terrorist organizations who ambushed them were labeled by the fake news as "peace keeping" organizations "on the side of angels", if you can believe that shit.

Assaults on white people and those who identified genders became commonplace in this warped version of reality. One had to arm oneself just to go out in public, in case you crossed paths with a mainstream media created zombie who might hurt you. You weren't allowed to say certain words or wear certain clothes or style your hair certain ways. The media had overstepped its boundaries much like the government who owned it had done, decades prior. They seemed as though they felt that they were above the law and any sense of divine reciprocity. Like cartoon characters, they thought they got away with it if lightning didn't immediately strike after committing an offense.

Kids stopped learning how to be productive and constructive and only knew how to destroy property and be nuisances that you didn't want to interact with. They forgot how to talk right. They no longer mastered the English language and talked in gibberish. The ability to pronounce the letter T in a word was sodomized right out of them. Important became "impor-ant" from the lips of a Millennial. Kids couldn't make food without making us sick, so we stopped eating out so much and saved money while eating more healthy. Kids all wanted to be rich but none of them had strong work ethics. Their role models and famous zheroes were feeble-minded parasites on the ass of society, often famous without the qualifying prerequisite that they be talented. We could tell which kids to avoid by what was blasting from their speakers. If they pulled up next to us at a traffic light, we clenched our gats and hoped to avoid becoming a news story..."Go on, little zombie fuck-fart, entertained by that ridiculous clown-shoes shit. Take your bitch ass on down the road and don't make me hafta' fire off on ya', yo."

Kids got to where they couldn't do the most basic of tasks. They became weak and sad and devoid of purpose. They seemed to have no sense of pride in their crafts. Jobs were just a place to get their checks from, to them. They didn't care if they made good pizzas or hamburgers or provided good service. All they cared about was social media, popularity, video games and getting fucked-up. Kids were unable to safely cross the street. They walked out into traffic while looking down at their slave-made iGadgets and got hit more and more often. Kids were programmed to be socially challenged, unable to hold an oral conversation, needing to text to accommodate their mainstream embedded insecurities. This resulted in those same kids being drivally challenged when they got behind the wheel, because those kids could not utilize a hands-free talking device because, well, they couldn't TALK on their PHONES.

Nothing in the world was safe from the kids programmed by the monster media. They raped statues and desecrated monuments. They raped the world, even spray painted all over any rocks and caves they encountered that they couldn't, otherwise, vandalize. They were programmed to leave negative instead of positive evidence of their passing through an area. They were programmed to shun their responsibility to nature to instead adopt a brutish, drunken junkie meth-head "power over nature" mentality. The females were programmed to want interracial sex and to turn their noses up at any males who may be educated, productive, or otherwise desirable to an intelligent woman. All good role models for kids were removed from the media and replaced with dregs and deadbeats. What was started with the permitting of the kidnappings had come to fruition. The taxpayers who were victimized by the crybaby lazy assed thugs who wouldn't get educations and jobs and work were somehow less important to the dumb-fuck generation. They didn't empathize with the good people until it was their turn to be victimized by the thugs they wanted coddled and enabled.

Kids got to where they couldn't be trusted with anything. Trusted with their bodies, they vandalized their own flesh with piercings and tattoos, scribbling all over themselves like ghetto-fabulous fucktards with no raising. These kids were spawn of the generation that was fans of the gangsta thug lazy crybaby kidnapper no-talent-having "rappers". These kids had the equivalent of no parents, just overgrown children who could be entertained by 3rd grade level bullshit, a thug crying about how bad HIS kind makes the 'hoods because they're too inferior to the taxpayers to join them and work for a living. Suddenly, there were kids who took the ghetto with them everywhere they'd go. It was becoming a generation of human-shaped wreckage and the main culprits were the celebs and sports zheroes who influenced the kids and the parents of the kids, before them.

So, one dumbed-down generation spawned another generation that's even more dumbed-down and brutish than they were. They were already impressionable, as they exhibited with their lack of good musical taste. Now their kids were intolerably retarded beyond comprehension. Underachievement had become the norm. Achievers were ridiculed and often snuffed out by this generation of parasites, extensions of the assholes of their fav famous celebs or sports zheroes. The world became unbearable for the intelligent, who had to watch the it all be destroyed by the retarded, who were controlled by the rich inbreds who owned the famous celebs and sports zheroes that they idolized.

There were no good famous people left to influence the kids, so the kids became vile and nasty, undesirable on all levels; covered in tattoos and poked full of disgusting holes. It was so sad to witness. The famous didn't possess the mental fortitude required to be ashamed at what their influence had created, neither. They continued to serve their subhuman masters who were High Priests to an ancient artificial intelligence that'd had humans build a mini version of itself to dominate the human paradigm. They were oblivious to their own zombification and thought that they were smarter than those who'd voted for Trump, although the opposite was the truth.

Chapter 5

Fake Education Fake History Fake Religion Fake News Fake Fakity Fake Fake Fake

During this clown-shoes disguised as humans era, there were 70 million homeless animals being ignored by all organized religious sects. There were 2.2 BILLION "Christians" who outnumbered the homeless animals. There were more than that in Muslims. There was no excuse for the unnecessary suffering that the animals endured at the hands of the merciless mainstream-created zombies. There wasn't even enough homeless animals to go around. But their preachers, teachers and pastors were nothing more than charlatans who didn't really care about the creations of their God. They cared about control, numbers and money. The same scribes who infiltrated the ancient temples and controlled the Bible and religion were still in control. The fake Jews who'd immigrated to Jerusalem and then cried out "Free Barabbas! Crucify Christ!" until the crowd joined them in the chant were even more in number and more powerful than ever before. Now, they could use that same method of operation, anywhere, and the humans would fall for it and credit it to the majority. It's all old ploys that still work, flawlessly.

One rich asshole can hire a few thuggish malcontents to go to a city to "protest" an issue to favor his agenda or mindset. They may be brainwashed enough to believe what they're saying, or they may just be beyond caring. If enough of the targeted demographic get exposed to the triggering, then the protest can grow into a riot and pillaging and make the news, which is also owned by the rich asshole. Then, the rich asshole's "news" programs present the story the way that the rich asshole wants it presented and the truth is never mentioned. Like a wizard behind a curtain, the rich asshole never gets punished for his treason. He walks away from molesting the mindset of the masses without even a slap on the wrist. Get a few rich assholes like that competing for power over the populations' perspective and you have propaganda wars, manipulated weather, devastation and civil unrest in every direction. Religious mindsets were not excluded from the targeting. No. In most cases, they were devolved, first. Even Christ battled them and cast a group of them from one (just one) of the temples. The issue Christ had with them was more than just "money changing".

Christians of this Trump-hate era were self-entitled assholes who had boats and expensive cars and big houses and pools and extra rooms and not one memory of helping a homeless animal or person, ever, with all of that blessing. They ran amok declaring their fake love for their God whose animals they ignored with every passing second. They lived by the same double standards as the world and its rich and famous zombies. They could never be imposed upon to do anything good, ever. But their feet would run quick to do something evil as fuck, every time. It seemed as though the world was doomed if this was exemplary of what "good" people are supposed to be. What happened to being the rescuing hands of Christ to those suffering unnecessarily? They served the world and its system that required the unnecessary suffering of all things to please the ancient AI...As long as they weren't the ones required to suffer, they were okay with it.

The other most prevalent religion was transformed into a weapon of the rich assholes who funded extreme militant terrorist groups who operated under the guise of doctrinal condoning. The rich assholes had agendas and plans for the world that involved depopulation and slavery and control of the paradigm of others. Their bloodlines had engaged in so much incestuous inbreeding to keep their lineages "pure" that they had become completely deranged. Their ancestors had written up letters and messages and texts of their evil plans to take Earth hostage. They held Satanic ceremonies that were actually anti-Satanic when you consider that his agendas oppose their agendas. As a good God of this world, Satan would want to be known for blessing all peoples and animals, and for selecting only those who'd best serve this agenda to be famous or wealthy or powerful. Satan would never choose the self-serving to be in power or to have wealth or influence in his world. They pretended to be Satanists while fighting against him and his will.

People were becoming ever more compliant in their newfound roles as zombies, avatars and bots to the ancient artificial intelligence. They were living contradictions of themselves and the values that they proclaimed to possess. If they spouted off about God or Allah, you knew you'd never see them rescuing homeless animals or making the world a better place for anyone other than themselves and other self-absorbed fucktards like them. They were engaged in class wars, seeing who could get the most "blessings". They dropped the ball on being the hands of God and lights of the world. It got so bad that you couldn't tell a "Christian" from a "Satanist". Both demographics were equally fake, hypocritical, good for nothing, self-serving, arrogant, boastful, dishonest, greedy, adulterous, lascivious and obediently branded for the AI with tattoos and piercings. None cared for the animals that God and Lucifer would have them rescuing. Few cared for homeless people. None cared to preserve the innocence of children. The secrets to generating the power to cause the miraculous were successfully hidden from this generation.

People were dumbed-down, had become utterly stupid. They believed complete bullshit and denied truth. They were entertained by what only the primitive would find entertaining. They were programmed to express when they don't like something so that they could be used as bots, later, via triggering. It started off innocently enough. They replaced a star system on the dominant video site with a thumbs up or down system as a programming tool. The star system had the supremacy of people remaining passive if they didn't like a video. But the thumbs up and down system was designed to test and to program people, like trained apes. Then, humans devolved further with a retarded mindset that went along with the thumbs up and down system: Suddenly, there were fucktards who thought that videos were being uploaded for their approval; so they watched them just to "rate" them with a thumbs up or down. They even made comments, like judges on a panel of a lame TV show, to accompany this fucktardation.

Even the educated had become dumb as fuck. "Professors" were teaching their students flat-out lies and fake history to make them trigger-able as waiting and reliable sleeper cells to do their bidding, later. Then, the dialog would change and become more aggressive, requiring "action" on the part of the students. Educators were now gestapo brain-washers who sent their pupils on missions of social unrest and violence against the innocent. They even stooped low enough to call for the deaths of entire demographics of people, including law enforcement. Professors wanted cops killed...unless that professor was being mugged, of course; THEN he'd want to see a living cop.

The stupidity we allowed to be passed-off as education was cartoonish, and then we wondered why the educated kids were so goddamned dumb. There was nowhere to turn for sanity and rational thought. Nobody on TV or radio was going to provide it. Nobody in any church was going to journey there. Craziness was the norm. Sane people were labeled by the insane and often targeted and victimized for daring to have clarity. To live safely among the zombies, one had to learn to publicly act like a zombie. You had to pretend to care about nonsensical bullshit to fit in with them. If your opinion differed from theirs, they reacted with aggression, labeling and, oftentimes, violence. They'd become inferior enough to expect respect that they never afforded to others. The majority seemed to be abiding by double standards that always benefited them. This was from teaching them to be self-serving at a young age. Those who cared about anything real, like homeless animals or people, were labeled as "freaks", isolated from the majority and were usually targeted.

Nothing real could be accessed anymore. It had become a world of fakeness. The news was fake for so long that nobody even noticed it was fake. Music was fake. Sports was fake. Their zheroes were fake as fuck; buncha' overgrown, good for nothing spoiled brats and bitches with too much money, fame and influence over the impressionable. Reality shows were scripted, dramatized, faked "reality". Everywhere you looked, you saw fakeness peeking through the mist. It was like a veil was lifted for some of us. We could "see" what was happening. We understood what was behind it all. But the majority had been botted, utilized as avatars and were totally oblivious to it.

Chapter 6

No Sound Doctrine...A Famine In The Land

There was a famine in the land for sanity and sound doctrine. Lines of reality had somehow been blurred and few seemed to have a grasp of what was real and what was not. Circus Science had prevailed over solid science and scientists were stealing all credibility away from it. Humans were still murdering animals for meat, even though they had the technology to create meat in labs that could be morphed into processing facilities. There was massive experimentation and poisoning occurring upon the majority of working class people via food and weather manipulation that none had consented to. Every other commercial ad on TV was for a drug that cured a man-caused ailment and there was no public outrage about it. The insults to injury were rubbed in our faces and we were too far gone in denial to accept the facts. People seemed to prefer LARP theater to actual reality, having become so accustomed to fakeness.

There were dramatic prophetic events that were ignored or distracted from. Nobody noticed the fulfillment of the "Prayer of Abomination" prophecy when it happened, for example. All real knowledge and accepted facts were being challenged as misinformation. People began to doubt what they knew to be true about almost everything. The ancient AI's little mini-me version of itself was dominating the collective human consciousness. Ripples were caused in space and time. Holes were punched into other timelines so the rich fucks could try to rape and pillage them like they did this one. Intervention was overdue because the fucked-up-edness was only gaining in momentum.

People got so stupid during the Obama administration that they actually became terrorists against a flag. Somehow, a bunch of zombies got botted into being triggered by the Dixie flag and associating it to racism. They were ignorant and uneducated morons who didn't know that true history reflects that many who were ANTI-slavery flew that flag while helping slaves escape to the Underground Railroad. Most people who flew the Dixie flag were ANTI-slavery, anti-establishment.

Fake history was never challenged. Few knew that Lincoln was actually a terrorist who worked for the Queen, who secretly ran America since 1776 like the wizard of Oz behind the curtain. Lincoln's true history, like that of hanging those who resisted the regime up by their thumbnails and taking their property, was never widely exposed or talked about. He was accepted as a "hero" who "freed the slaves". No regard for the fact that he only released the slaves as what he perceived would be a terrorist attack, not realizing that there were more anti-slavery people in the south than pro-slavery. You see, slaves were only owned by rich fucks (white AND Black). Poor folks didn't like their jobs being taken away by murderers (who were sentenced to death by good African Black people) who were then shipped in and given amnesty in exchange for free labor. That's something that was kept hidden so that the majority of Blacks would remain trigger-able with racial bullshit whenever they needed to stage a social uprising. There's a huge thing you can pull off by changing the descriptive of a "prisoner" ship to what they're called in "history" books. You can perpetuate atrocities and never get checked for that shit.

All recorded doctrine was changed, somehow, and the prophecy regarding the famine in the land manifested. People noticed changes in scriptures, words that were never there before, stuff like that. The exposure of many charlatans happened due to this, as they continued to read the altered text without any reference to what it once conveyed. They didn't have any of the content committed to heart (memory) and therefore didn't seem to know the difference between the original and the fake. They would read the verses and leave their followers in the dark brought on by the changes. Stumbling-blocks were created out of what were once brilliant teachers.

Hypocrisy and underachievement were glamorized, after their appointed time of being normalized. A double standard was perpetuated to sexualize children, for years, on international TV: As long as the perp was female, she could make your kids have to think about sex whenever they saw her because she was allowed to talk about her sexuality in front of your kids. Heterosexual men would be vilified for the same behavior, of course, especially if they were white. But lesbians were allowed to be child-sexualizing public pedophiles without scrutiny and even make millions for doing it. This caused a downward spiral of morality that never bottomed out because a new low was always reached just when you thought it couldn't get any worse.

Chapter 7

Bullying Gender Assaulting Sex

The rich fucks funded a lot of Circus Science to increase their incomes with "treatment" for the diseases and illnesses they caused. There seemed to be no line that those inbreds wouldn't cross. In addition to using science to cause health and psychiatric problems for profit, the rich fucks also engaged in "sport" assaults on sexuality and sex, itself. They caused people to have a wide barrage of sex related health issues. They even attacked anal sex (proving that they're fake/not real Satanists) with food DNA manipulations and self-emulating nanobots. The self-emulating nanobots that they sprayed in the sky had a version that went into the food and into the bodies of those who ate it. These little monster nanobots could get into a tendon, vein or muscle and multiply themselves until they caused horrible excruciating pain.

The rich fucks didn't always attack just sexual function. They often caused unexplainable pain in peoples' bodies that doctors would appear to be unable to diagnose and properly treat. Traditional pain medication, on its own, was usually useless against these pains caused by the nanobots. One would have to enhance the effects of the prescribed pain medications with the heavy use of Marijuana just to obtain any measurable level of relief. People who didn't smoke Marijuana were being stricken with various forms of Cancer at higher rates than smokers were. The rich fucks didn't want any of their puppet politicians to back the Constitution of the United States of America, which protects the legality of Marijuana and its use, because it'd cut into their healthcare and pharmaceutical profits. Peoples' rights were being violated and they didn't rally or rise up in anger over it. But they could be triggered to rape a statue or burn down a city in rages over non-issues.

Part of the depopulation agenda obviously required an assault on gender, itself. Young people were being programmed to deny their gender and the very functionality of it, entirely. Little boys were no longer called "boys". It was becoming illegal to refer to someone as any gender descriptive. Calling the wrong woman a "woman" or "female" could result in horrible public outrage, backlash, assaults and even sabotage of income to feed one's family. Freedom of speech was assaulted, on all levels. The rich fucks dictated the accepted dialect and vocabulary of the masses, especially the whites. White people were under genocidal assault. The other races wanted fine white ass to fuck, but they were stupid enough to want to wipe out the supply of that booty, like retards who burn their source trees.

To expect anything normal of anyone was becoming an offense that could hurt someone's feelings, which was also becoming illegal to do. Men were no longer MEN who could do morning chores, eat breakfast, go to work, return from work to do more chores (man stuff) and interact with their families. No. They became these useless zombified robots, ever more obedient to the ancient AI and far less human than the men of previous generations. They needed to have their feeble little minds entertained by violence, sports, illicit sex and other taboo shit. Family values were cast to the wayside. Most families didn't even get together for breakfast and dinner. There was no structure or stability to hold people together. Technology and social media had sucked the spirit out of people and they were willingly dumbed down and compliant to the will of the rich fucks. They didn't seem to notice nor care that they allowed their own wives and kids to be robbed of the better men that they could be if they'd just try to be a little bit more old school and original and stop trying to fit in with the wrong majority.

It got hard to communicate with other people. You had to be very careful what you said or you might cause a zombie fit. Coddling of those who were wrong and deserving of rebuke became the norm under the perverse double standards that we were all expected to abide by. Weak leadership resulted in weak masses. Men were weak and girly and constantly shunning their manly responsibilities, as if fairies would magically appear to replace them and be the masculine men that they were refusing to be. Women who were heterosexual wanted heterosexual guys after making themselves masculine with piercings and tattoos to the extreme that only someone attracted to guys would find them attractive. Their refusal to reject the retardation of the ancient AI was causing them to sabotage themselves and their futures. They scribbled on their bodies because the AI couldn't stand how beautiful they were, naturally, and so programmed them to do it. Then, they wanted to be as desirable to heterosexual men as they were before they made their arms more masculine than their boyfriends' arms. It was so sad to witness.

So it looked like the end for the white race at the time of this writing. If you were white, the whole world hated you, including other whites who'd been botted by them to be self-loathing. White women were being programmed to reject white men as too inferior to be worthy of their sexuality. Whites were blaming "all whites" for all of the problems in the world, even in places where there were no whites to perpetuate the violence that was so prevalent in those areas (yet, somehow, "White Supremacists" were still somehow responsible for that Black on Black violence). Whites were afraid to speak-up for themselves, and those who did found it to be futile and even deadly.

So little white kids were the most deprived of rights of all in this era when they couldn't be boys nor girls nor white without facing persecution for it. The rich fucks had not only attacked sexuality, but they attempted to wipe-out an entire race in the process. They did succeed in making it miserable for most whites to exist on the planet, which was a victory for them, in itself.

Chapter 8

What's Left To Censor

We were enduring assaults against intelligence, truth and knowledge and the very concept of civilization. The rich fucks had gained control of the airwaves and chased out the good people in music who'd protect the gates from the likes of Madonna and those to follow once she got the bar dropped low enough to accept her as mainstream. They controlled sports and the news and all other facets of the entertainment industry. The last resistance to their complete control of mass perspective was the internet. The rich fucks gained control of the internet and set about censoring it of all content disputing their permissible mass perspective. They hired trolls to attack content providers and set computer algorithms against them. They used technology to identify and squelch out all who dared defy them and their agendas. Voice recognition came in handy to rob content providers of view counts and of showing up in related video columns. People were programmed to reject content not already viewed many times, so low view counts kept their most controlled zombies away from those videos.

There were content providers who had videos demonetized and their youtube channels were removed for daring to share an opposing opinion to mainstream provided misinformation. Users who shared truth, in any capacity, were trolled, discredited, persecuted, bullied and censored into oblivion. Those real truthers were unable to live stream videos and their view counts were always lower than the videos were actually viewed. Some giveaways would be a video that's been liked 200 plus times and thumbs downed 50 times while only showing 37 views, which happened a lot on youtube after the takeover by the rich fucks.

Online sabotage of income became the norm for the rich fucks, like a perverse sport. They would target someone they didn't like and cause their revenue online to dissipate into nothing. Their book and mp3 sales would dwindle. Their videos would stop making money. Sometimes, a content provider would have a video demonetized while it was hot, being viewed a lot. Then, when the view counts per day dropped, the video would magically be monetized again. Underground music artists who were targeted were the subjects of regular sabotage as their content would mysteriously never make it to the retailer website for perusal and sale. There were many ploys and methods for sucking the wind out of the sails of the true resistance, who didn't have huge followings nor lots of subscribers, so nobody even knew they were there. The "resistance" that had millions of subscribers and lots of video view counts and was able to live stream was CONTROLLED resistance, they never crossed the lines drawn by the rich fucks.

Censoring of content has gotten so bad that I'm apprehensive about writing this book and investing any time in it. I'm writing this because I'm frustrated. I've witnessed so much carnage against Trump and us and the nation by the famous fuckfarts that I feel that they should pay for my therapy if they ever went on TV to subject me to their treasonous Trump-hate bullshit. I hope that lots of people buy this book as a statement that they're fuckin' tired of this shit, too. I hope it makes number one on the sell list and snuffs out What Happened, not because it's especially good or because I'm a good writer, which it's not and I'm not. But because they want us to be isolated and frustrated and broke and I'm one of those people whose income got snuffed out by them. High sales of this long, drawn-out rant would be the ultimate statement that they are NOT winning and they will NEVER win against us. We WILL find each other and rescue each other from them and the pits of deprivation that they've tossed us into.

One final thought in closing:

They've hit some of us with manic depression. We're not really suicidal, but we're really sad most of the time. They know that this works with whatever it is that they hit us with to raise our blood pressure, to spike it even higher. It's an attempt on your life. Recognize it and apply the mind control techniques that the Clone of Yah, Jesus Christ, taught His followers. He said to think on whatsoever is pure, just and of good report, in so many words. He meant to think positively and to envelop yourself in an invisible bubble of positive energy to enhance the ability for good things to happen for and to you, supernaturally. You can fight the negative thoughts by refusing to think them and replacing them with positive thoughts of your own. You can refuse to be triggered by any external influence or event or media or "news" bytes. You can choose to commandeer your own mind to manifest the environment that YOU desire rather than being an avatar to create an atmosphere that the rich fucks want for you.

If you want to medicate for your depression, good Sativas will hit the spot better than any pharmaceutical (sorcery of man) or alcoholic beverage (alcohol is a depressant). As someone who battles extreme manic depression on the suicide level, I can tell you from experience that most bouts with this man-manipulated psychological disorder can be won by you. You're not really here to be happy so much as to fulfill a purpose, anyway. But being happy along the way encourages more good things to happen that can make you even more happy. It can become an empowering circle that cycles out almost regularly to enable you to benefit others with the crumbs from your table (your excess). Your own empowerment may have ripple effects that benefit someone or something that would've been neglected without that turn of events...

So you should strive to be positive, since it's what they don't want you to be. Now you understand who and what "they" are and you're better equipped to defeat them at their own game.

Peace. I'm out.